DO-IT-AGAIN ROCK CYCLE

by Rex Ruby

Minneapolis, Minnesota

Credits
Cover and title page, © Skynavin/Shutterstock, © GP PHOTOTRENDS/Shutterstock, © Yvonne Baur/ Shutterstock, © Sanya Kushak/iStock, and © Andrey_Kuzmin/iStock; 4–5, © Tpopova/iStock; 5, © simonkr/iStock; 6, © HAYKIRDI/iStock; 7T, © aleks-p/Adobe Stock; 7M, © michal812/Shutterstock; 7B, © Pannarai/Adobe Stock; 8T, © www.sandatlas.org/Shutterstock; 8B, © vvoe/Shutterstock; 9, © Shutterstock; 10, © coffmancmu/Adobe Stock; 11, © Mateusz/Adobe Stock; 12, © JadeThaiCatwalk/iStock; 13, © Shutterstock; 14, © samopauser/ Adobe Stock; 15, © Shutterstock; 17, © Shutterstock; 18–19, © Noradoa/Adobe Stock; 20, © chaiyapruek2520/ iStock; 21T, © Beboy_ltd/iStock; 21TR, © www.sandatlas.org/Shutterstock; 21BR, © Shutterstock; 21B, © www. sandatlas.org/Shutterstock; 21BL, © Shutterstock; 21TL, © Keith Levit/Shutterstock; 22, © matty2x4/iStock, © Brillianata/iStock, © studiocasper/iStock, © kyoshino/iStock, and © Brillianata/iStock.

Bearport Publishing Company Product Development Team
President: Jen Jenson; Director of Product Development: Spencer Brinker; Managing Editor: Allison Juda; Associate Editor: Naomi Reich; Associate Editor: Tiana Tran; Art Director: Colin O'Dea; Designer: Kim Jones; Designer: Kayla Eggert; Product Development Assistant: Owen Hamlin

STATEMENT ON USAGE OF GENERATIVE ARTIFICIAL INTELLIGENCE
Bearport Publishing remains committed to publishing high-quality nonfiction books. Therefore, we restrict the use of generative AI to ensure accuracy of all text and visual components pertaining to a book's subject. See BearportPublishing.com for details.

Library of Congress Cataloging-in-Publication Data is available at www.loc.gov or upon request from the publisher.

ISBN: 979-8-89232-027-6 (hardcover)
ISBN: 979-8-89232-504-2 (paperback)
ISBN: 979-8-89232-156-3 (ebook)

Copyright © 2025 Bearport Publishing Company. All rights reserved. No part of this publication may be reproduced in whole or in part, stored in any retrieval system, or transmitted in any form or by any means, electronic, mechanical, photocopying, recording, or otherwise, without written permission from the publisher. Bearport Publishing is a division of Chrysalis Education Group.

For more information, write to Bearport Publishing, 5357 Penn Avenue South, Minneapolis, MN 55419.

CONTENTS

Forming Rocks. 4
Three Main Types 6
Forming Igneous Rock. 8
Rock from Volcanoes. 10
Changing to Sediment. 12
Making Sedimentary Rock 14
Changing to Metamorphic Rock 16
Melting to Magma 18
Always Changing 20

Science Lab. 22
Glossary 23
Index. 24
Read More 24
Learn More Online 24
About the Author 24

FORMING ROCKS

From sandy beaches to tall mountains, rocks are all around us. Most of these rocks are millions of years old. However, that doesn't mean they always stay the same. In fact, old rocks are changing into new rocks all the time. The processes of old rocks turning into new ones is called the **rock cycle**.

There are thousands of different kinds of rocks on Earth.

THREE MAIN TYPES

Scientists group Earth's rocks into three main types. There are **igneous** (IG-nee-uhs), **sedimentary** (*sed*-uh-MEN-tur-ee), and **metamorphic** (*met*-uh-MOR-fik) rocks. Each type forms in different ways, and new igneous, sedimentary, and metamorphic rocks are being created all the time. The rock cycle never stops. It is always changing rocks from one kind into another.

Geology is the scientific study of Earth. Scientists who study rocks are called geologists.

FORMING IGNEOUS ROCK

Igneous rock can form in two different ways. The first happens inside Earth's rocky **crust**. Deep underground, there is superhot liquid rock called **magma**. Sometimes, this liquid rock oozes up into cracks in the crust. When the magma cools, it hardens into igneous rock.

Gabbro

Pegmatite

Gabbro (GAB-broh) and pegmatite (peg-MUH-tite) are two igneous rocks that form inside Earth's crust.

How Igneous Rock Forms

Magma that has cooled to become igneous rock

Earth's crust

Earth's crust

Magma oozing into crust

ROCK FROM VOLCANOES

Igneous rock can also form on Earth's surface. Sometimes, a large crack breaks through the surface—this is called a volcano. Then, magma rises out and onto the land above. Once it does, the hot liquid rock is called lava. As the lava cools and hardens, it turns into igneous rock.

These holes are made from the gas in the lava.

Pumice (PUHM-is) is an igneous rock that forms from lava that is full of gas.

The thicker the lava, the longer it takes to cool into solid rock.

CHANGING TO SEDIMENT

Rain and wind can change igneous rock into a new type of rock. How does this happen? When it rains, water flows down larger rocks and loosens pieces, eventually breaking them off. These small, free pieces of rock are called **sediment**. Sediment gets washed away from the bigger rock. Sometimes, it may go into a river.

Mud, pebbles, and sand are all types of sediments.

MAKING SEDIMENTARY ROCK

Sediment is carried along by wind or water. Sometimes, a flowing river moves the little rocky pieces to a bigger body of water, such as a lake. Sediment settles at the bottom. Then, over millions of years, the sediment builds up. Layer by layer, the tiny rocky pieces join together to become sedimentary rock.

Conglomerate

Conglomerate (kuhn-GLOM-uh-rit) is a sedimentary rock made up of differently sized pieces of sediment.

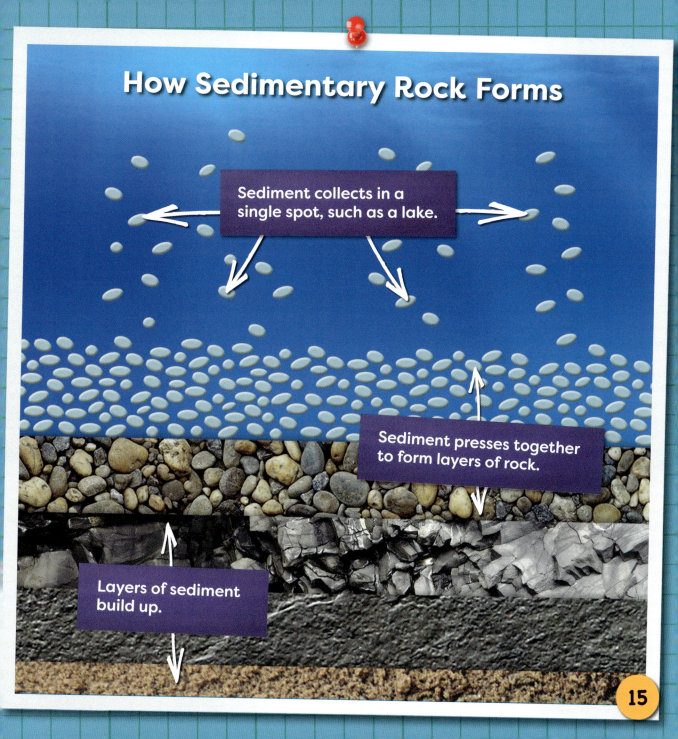

CHANGING TO METAMORPHIC ROCK

Sedimentary rock doesn't stay the same forever either. It can turn into metamorphic rock. When Earth's crust cracks and moves, rocks are crushed, stretched, and folded against one another. These movements create lots of **pressure** and heat. This bakes and crushes the sedimentary rock into metamorphic rock.

The cracks in Earth's crust caused by movement are called faults.

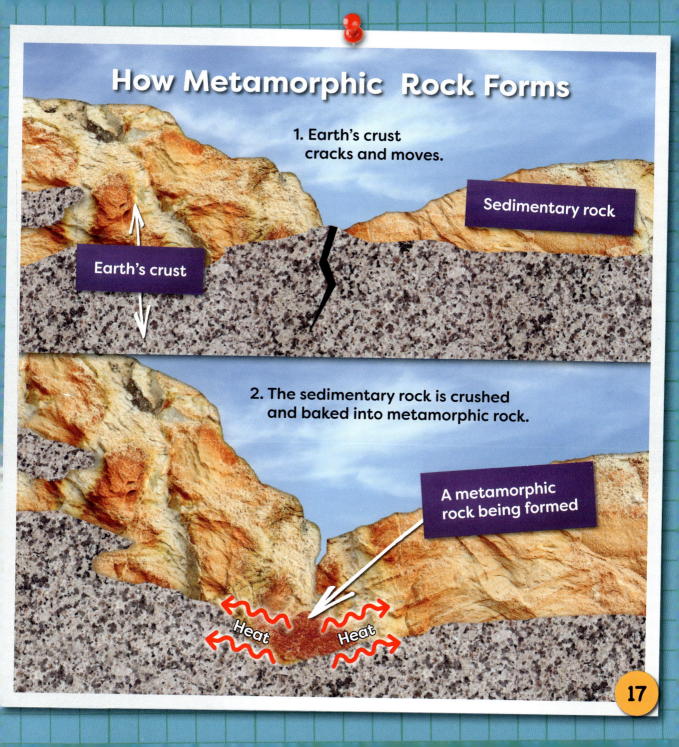

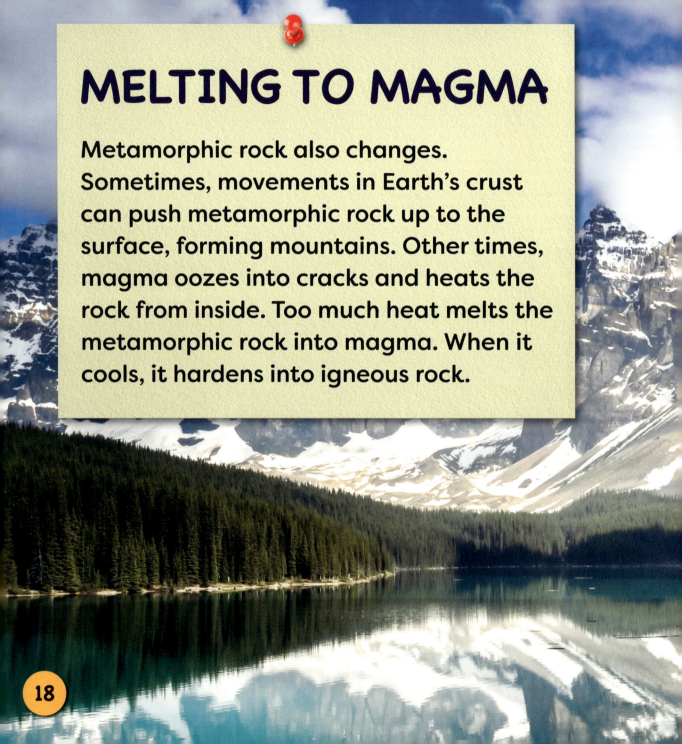

MELTING TO MAGMA

Metamorphic rock also changes. Sometimes, movements in Earth's crust can push metamorphic rock up to the surface, forming mountains. Other times, magma oozes into cracks and heats the rock from inside. Too much heat melts the metamorphic rock into magma. When it cools, it hardens into igneous rock.

The Rocky Mountains in Colorado are made of mostly metamorphic rock.

Over time, mountains can break down into sediment and form sedimentary rock.

ALWAYS CHANGING

Rocks have been changing from one type to another for billions of years. The rock cycle can happen in any order. Given the right conditions and enough time, one rock can become just about any other. In fact, it's happening right now!

There are old rocks around today that dinosaurs once stood upon!

The Rock Cycle

See some of the ways old rocks become new rocks.

Magma erupts from a volcano as lava.

Lava cools and hardens into igneous rock.

Rainwater breaks down igneous rock into sediment.

Built-up layers of sediment form sedimentary rock.

Sedimentary rock is baked into metamorphic rock.

Metamorphic rock melts and becomes magma.

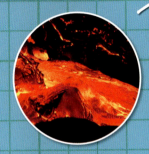

SCIENCE LAB

Make a Model of the Rock Cycle

Use what you have learned to make a model showing how old rocks change into new rocks during the rock cycle.

You will need:
- Paper
- Markers
- Scissors
- A large piece of cardboard

1. Draw a volcano and lava on some paper.

2. Next, draw igneous, sedimentary, and metamorphic rocks. Make some sediment.

3. Cut out all your parts of the rock cycle.

4. Arrange your rocks on the cardboard in an order in which they might go through the rock cycle.

5. Cut out arrows and place them between your steps to show the cycle changing one kind of rock to the next.

6. Label the different kinds of rock in your model.

GLOSSARY

crust the hard outer layer of rock that forms Earth's surface

geology the study of Earth's rocks

igneous rock that forms from magma or lava that has cooled and become solid

magma hot liquid rock beneath the surface of Earth

metamorphic rock that forms when rock is put under high heat or pressure

pressure the force made by pushing down or pressing on something

rock cycle the process in which one type of rock changes to become a new type of rock

sediment tiny pieces of rock that have broken away from larger rocks

sedimentary rock that forms from layers of tiny pieces of rock

INDEX

crust 8–10, 16–18
geologists 6
geology 6
igneous rock 6–10, 12, 18, 21–22
lake 14–15
lava 10–11, 21–22
magma 8–10, 18, 21
metamorphic rock 6–7, 16–19, 21–22
rain 12, 21
river 12–14
rock cycle 4, 6, 20–22
sediment 12–15, 21–22
sedimentary rock 6–7, 14–17, 19, 21–22
volcano 10–11, 21–22

READ MORE

Gieseke, Tyler. *The Rock Cycle (Earth Cycles)*. Minneapolis: DiscoverRoo, 2023.

McDougal, Anna. *The Rock Cycle (Earth's Rocks in Review)*. Buffalo, NY: Enslow Publishing, 2024.

LEARN MORE ONLINE

1. Go to **www.factsurfer.com** or scan the QR code below.
2. Enter "**Rockin Rock Cycle**" into the search box.
3. Click on the cover of this book to see a list of websites.

ABOUT THE AUTHOR

Rex Ruby lives in Minnesota with his family. He likes going on long walks and discovering new rocks along the trail.